GLOBAL EFFECTS

THE IMPACT OF SCIENCE, TECHNOLOGY, AND ECONOMICS IN THE UNITED STATES AND CANADA

J.M. KLEIN

Boulder City Library
701 Adams Blvd.
Boulder City, NV 89005

PowerKiDS press

Published in 2021 by The Rosen Publishing Group, Inc.
29 East 21st Street, New York, NY 10010

Copyright © 2021 by The Rosen Publishing Group, Inc.

All rights reserved. No part of this book may be reproduced in any form without permission in writing from the publisher, except by a reviewer.

First Edition

Editor: Siyavush Saidian
Book Design: Tanya Dellaccio

Photo Credits: Cover Justin Sullivan/Getty Images News/Getty Images; p. 5 (top) Robert Kneschke/Shutterstock.com; p. 5 (bottom) https://upload.wikimedia.org/wikipedia/commons/7/79/Countries_by_GDP_%28Nominal%29_in_2014.svg; p. 7 (top) i viewfinder/Shutterstock.com; p. 7 (bottom) George Rose/Getty Images News/Getty Images; p. 9 (top) Klanarong Chitmung/Shutterstock.com; p. 9 (bottom) Steve Heap/Shutterstock.com; p. 11 PhilAugustavo/iStock'Getty Images Plus/Getty Images; p. 13 SOPA Images/LightRocket/Getty Images; p. 15 Bloomberg/Getty Images; p. 16 https://upload.wikimedia.org/wikipedia/commons/7/74/U.S._manufacturing_employment.png; p. 17 andresr/E+/Getty Images; p. 19 Walter Bibikow/DigitalVision/Getty Images; p. 21 (top) Stephen Brashear/Getty Images News/Getty Images; p. 21 (bottom) Science & Society Picture Library/SSPL/Getty Images; p. 22 Hulton Archive/Getty Images; p. 23 Jess Kraft/Shutterstock.com; p. 25 Galerie Bilderwelt/Hulton Archive/Getty Images; p. 27 Authenticated News/Archive Photos/Getty Images; p. 29 Alex Wong/Getty Images News/Getty Images.

Cataloging-in-Publication Data
 Names: Klein, J.M.
Title: The impact of science, technology, and economics in the United States and Canada / J.M. Klein.
Description: New York : PowerKids Press, 2021. | Series: Global effects | Includes glossary and index.
Identifiers: ISBN 9781725322240 (pbk.) | ISBN 9781725322264 (library bound) | ISBN 9781725322257 (6 pack) | ISBN 9781725322271 (ebook)
Subjects: LCSH: North America–Juvenile literature. | North America–Economic conditions–Juvenile literature. | Technology–North America. | Science–North America.
Classification: LCC E38.5 K545 2020 | DDC 917–dc23

Manufactured in the United States of America

CPSIA Compliance Information: Batch #CSPK20: For Further Information contact Rosen Publishing, New York, New York at 1-800-237-9932

CONTENTS

POWERFUL ECONOMIES 4
THE FREE ENTERPRISE SYSTEM 6
ECONOMIC FREEDOM 8
ABUNDANT NATURAL RESOURCES 10
A STEADY STREAM OF LABOR 12
EXCELLENCE IN ENTREPRENEURSHIP 14
A DOMINANT SERVICE INDUSTRY 16
A CHANGING RETAIL INDUSTRY 18
THE IMPORTANCE OF MANUFACTURING 20
MOVING AWAY FROM AGRICULTURE 22
SCIENTIFIC DISCOVERIES 24
TRADE AND COMMUNICATION 26
ETHICS AND THE ECONOMY 28
GLOSSARY 30
FOR MORE INFORMATION 31
INDEX 32

POWERFUL ECONOMIES

Freedom is an important concept to U.S. and Canadian citizens—and it applies to the economic systems of both countries. Americans and Canadians value freedom of choice, which has had a major impact on how both countries have grown.

Today, both the United States and Canada are in the top ten economic countries of the world. Both are also leaders in scientific and technological **innovations**. The United States and Canada are among the world's richest nations and have some of the strongest economies.

The United States is often considered to be the most technologically advanced country in the world—with the most technologically powerful economy. The U.S. dollar is the most-used currency in international transactions. It's the standard of currency in international markets for important products like gold and petroleum.

FAST FACT

SEVERAL COUNTRIES BESIDES THE UNITED STATES USE THE U.S. DOLLAR AS THEIR OFFICIAL CURRENCY, INCLUDING NATIONS IN SOUTH AMERICA, AFRICA, AND THE PACIFIC.

THE UNITED STATES HAS A STRONG ECONOMY AND ITS DOLLAR IS A RESPECTED CURRENCY AROUND THE WORLD.

STRONG GDPs

The United States is the world's largest overall economy in terms of **gross domestic product** (GDP), reaching an estimated $21.4 trillion in 2019. Despite its wealth, however, the United States does not have the highest per capita GDP. "Per capita" means "per person." It ranked tenth in the world in 2019 with a per capita GDP of around $60,000. Canada had an overall GDP of $1.91 trillion in 2019, with a per capita GDP of around $46,000.

COUNTRIES BY GDP (2014)

THE FREE ENTERPRISE SYSTEM

American and Canadian businesses are free from strict government control, operating under a minimal amount of **regulations**. Prices go up or down because of supply and demand, not because the government changes them. Private companies compete for **profit** without the government's supervision.

This type of economic structure is called a **free enterprise** system. Unlike **socialism** or **communism**, in which the government owns either some or all of the economic resources, free enterprise allows individuals or companies to own private **property**. That includes everything from land to **manufacturing** plants.

Under communism, the government also makes all the economic decisions. Under a free enterprise system, it's up to the consumers to determine whether a business succeeds or fails because they are free to decide how to spend their money.

MANUFACTURING: BUSINESSES THAT PRODUCE CONSUMER PRODUCTS.

FREE ENTERPRISE: AN ECONOMIC SYSTEM CHARACTERIZED BY FREEDOM FOR CONSUMERS AND PRODUCERS.

FAST FACT

LIFE EXPECTANCY IS CONNECTED TO A NATION'S ECONOMIC STRENGTH. IN 2019, AVERAGE LIFE EXPECTANCY IN THE UNITED STATES WAS 78.5 YEARS; IN CANADA, IT WAS 82.8 YEARS.

CANADA'S POLICIES: SIMILAR BUT DIFFERENT

While Canada has a free market economy overall, the government is more hands-on in Canada than it is in the United States. The Canadian government plays a large role in regulating and **subsidizing** Canadian industries. The government also owns and controls some of the country's resources. It owns the Canadian National Railway—one of the country's two railroads—and the Canadian Broadcasting Corporation, the country's national chain of public television stations. The Canadian government also owns and operates many public utilities.

THE CANADIAN GOVERNMENT OWNS AND CONTROLS SOME OF THE COUNTRY'S RESOURCES, INCLUDING THE CANADIAN NATIONAL RAILWAY.

ECONOMIC FREEDOM

Generally, Americans and Canadians have economic freedom. That is the ability to make personal decisions about what they want to do with their money and other economic resources. They can make a profit, decide how they want to provide their own labor (own a business or work for someone else), and find opportunities to invent and innovate. These are some benefits of a modern free enterprise system, often called capitalism.

Economic freedom in private businesses is a central feature in the culture of the United States and Canada. Low levels of regulation and government involvement mean that private companies make most of the decisions about what and how much the economy produces. However, the economy may sometimes weaken as a result of poor decisions by companies. This is one risk of capitalism.

FAST FACT

THE NEW YORK STOCK EXCHANGE IS MORE THAN THREE TIMES LARGER THAN ANY OTHER STOCK EXCHANGE IN THE WORLD. THE U.S. STOCK MARKET PLAYS AN INFLUENTIAL ROLE IN INTERNATIONAL FINANCE.

THE FEDERAL RESERVE'S LOGO IS ON THE $50 BILL.

THE UNITED STATES FEDERAL RESERVE SETS INTEREST RATES AS A WAY TO INFLUENCE THE AMERICAN ECONOMY—BUT NOT CONTROL IT.

GOVERNMENT INFLUENCE, NOT CONTROL

When an economy weakens, **recession** and **inflation** can lead to high unemployment and skyrocketing prices. But in a free enterprise system, the U.S. government can't set prices or control the supply of goods. Instead, the government influences the economy through trade and money policies. In 1913, the United States created a central bank called the Federal Reserve System. This bank can change interest rates, which affect the cost and profit of borrowing and lending money.

ABUNDANT NATURAL RESOURCES

The land in both Canada and the United States is rich in mineral resources, alongside fertile, or rich, farmland and widespread waterways that create shipping lanes.

Canada has the third-largest oil reserves in the world and it is the world's fifth-largest oil producer. It's the world leader in the production of many natural resources, including gold, nickel, uranium, diamonds, and petroleum, with an estimated $33.2 trillion worth of natural resources. The country is also a top supplier of natural gas and ranks third in exporting (or selling) timber to other countries.

The United States has some of the world's largest coal reserves, and mining is a major industry in the country. As a result, the United States is a world leader in coal production. Some $45 trillion in natural resources can be found in the country, including timber, copper, gold, oil, and natural gas deposits.

FAST FACT

CANADA HAS THE WORLD'S LONGEST COASTLINE. EASY ACCESS TO THE SEA HAS HELPED THE COUNTRY DEVELOP ONE OF THE WORLD'S LARGEST COMMERCIAL FISHING AND SEAFOOD INDUSTRIES.

THOUGH SOME CONSIDER COAL AN OUTDATED ENERGY SOURCE, IT'S STILL A MAJOR U.S. INDUSTRY.

RESOURCES HELP DETERMINE GROWTH

An abundance of natural resources influenced the growth of the United States and Canada. Both countries are important sources of oil and gas, leading to their success in vehicle production. The large amount of coal in the United States helped it grow during the Industrial Revolution, when coal powered much of the world. Canada's energy is cheap to produce due to the country's natural resources, and it is one of the highest per capita consumers of energy.

A STEADY STREAM OF LABOR

Immigration in the United States and Canada has played a key role in the development of these countries, in both the labor force and scientific discovery.

The continuously high number of **immigrants** to Canada and the United States means both countries have a steady supply of labor. The large number of available workers contribute to economic expansion, driving more people to come to these countries, which leads to further expansion. Today, both the United States and Canada have large, skilled labor forces.

The strength of technological innovations in both countries also benefits the labor market, because advanced technology leads to increased productivity.

Currently, the U.S. labor force is facing competition from other countries. It is often cheaper for companies to send jobs to countries like India and China, reducing the need for American workers.

FAST FACT
MORE THAN 1 MILLION IMMIGRANTS ARRIVE IN THE UNITED STATES EACH YEAR. ABOUT 1 IN 5 CANADIANS ARE IMMIGRANTS.

IMMIGRATION AND SCIENCE

Immigrants to the United States and Canada often bring new skills and ideas, which leads to scientific discovery. Scottish-born Alexander Graham Bell, the inventor of the first working telephone, moved to Canada in 1870, then to the United States in 1871. Nikola Tesla, who pioneered the alternating current electric system still used today, moved from Serbia in 1884. Albert Einstein, who would go on to develop many important theories, was one of many scientists from Germany who sought safety in the United States before World War II.

A STEADY AND CONSTANT FLOW OF IMMIGRANTS MEANS THE UNITED STATES HAS ALWAYS HAD A RELIABLE LABOR FORCE.

EXCELLENCE IN ENTREPRENEURSHIP

With its emphasis on innovation and its highly productive citizens, the United States excels in entrepreneurship, or people creating their own businesses. In 2015, studies found that around 27 million Americans were starting or running new businesses. Entrepreneurs in the United States generate 65 percent of all new jobs.

Most American entrepreneurs operate small businesses. The United States has around 30 million small businesses, which employ 47.5 percent of American workers. Small businesses find funding in the United States easier than other countries because of **venture capital**. This allows a private investor to fund a business in exchange for a stake in that business.

Entrepreneurship in Canada also plays a role in the country's economy. About 13 percent of Canadians are entrepreneurs, and the country ranks second in the world in levels of entrepreneurial activity.

FAST FACT
SEVERAL OF THE LARGEST COMPANIES AND EMPLOYERS IN THE WORLD ARE AMERICAN COMPANIES, INCLUDING WALMART AND MCDONALD'S.

THE IMPACT OF ENTREPRENEURS

American entrepreneurs make a global impact. From Henry Ford's automobile company to Steve Jobs's Apple technology company, American entrepreneurship has shaped the way people around the planet communicate and travel. Other celebrated American entrepreneurs include Vera Wang, Bill Gates, and Oprah Winfrey. Important Canadian entrepreneurs include Mike Lazaridis, the founder of Blackberry; John Molson, the founder of Molson Brewery; and Garrett Camp, the cofounder of Uber.

APPLE COFOUNDER AND AMERICAN ENTREPRENEUR STEVE JOBS HELPED REVOLUTIONIZE MODERN TECHNOLOGY WITH THE DEVELOPMENT OF THE iPHONE.

A DOMINANT SERVICE INDUSTRY

While both countries have a strong history in manufacturing and agriculture, today, the bulk of American and Canadian jobs are in service. People are leaving behind the factories and farms of their past and moving to service industry jobs.

Huge numbers of American and Canadian workers are employed in service industries. Three-quarters of Canadians work in the service industry, which generates 70 percent of Canada's GDP. In 2019, 71 percent of Americans—some 108 million people—worked in **service industries**. That's especially true in big cities like New York and Toronto where many residents work in service. Jobs in these industries are expected to continue to grow.

Pay rates in service industries vary. While jobs in finance and health care can be high paying, jobs in food service typically don't pay as well.

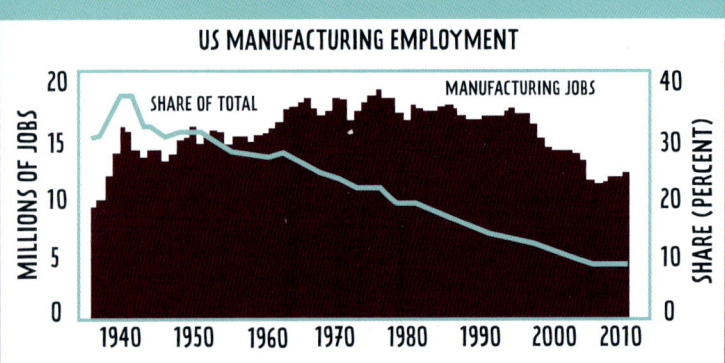

FAST FACT

THE U.S. BUREAU OF LABOR STATISTICS PROJECTS THE LABOR FORCE TO REACH 163.8 MILLION PEOPLE IN 2024. THE CANADIAN LABOR FORCE HIT AN ESTIMATED 19 MILLION PEOPLE IN 2018.

A VARIETY OF JOBS

Service job opportunities are both vast and **diverse**. Topping the list are specialized trade professions like electricians or carpenters. Also important are finance jobs (bankers, stockbrokers, and real estate agents), jobs in education (teachers, professors, and librarians), food and retail jobs (cooks and grocery store clerks), and transportation jobs. Jobs in health care—doctors, nurses, and assistants—are growing in the United States and Canada. In Canada, health care is the third-largest employer.

SERVICE INDUSTRIES: BUSINESSES THAT PROVIDE LABOR-INTENSIVE WORK RATHER THAN PRODUCING A PRODUCT.

DIVERSE: DIFFERENT OR VARIED.

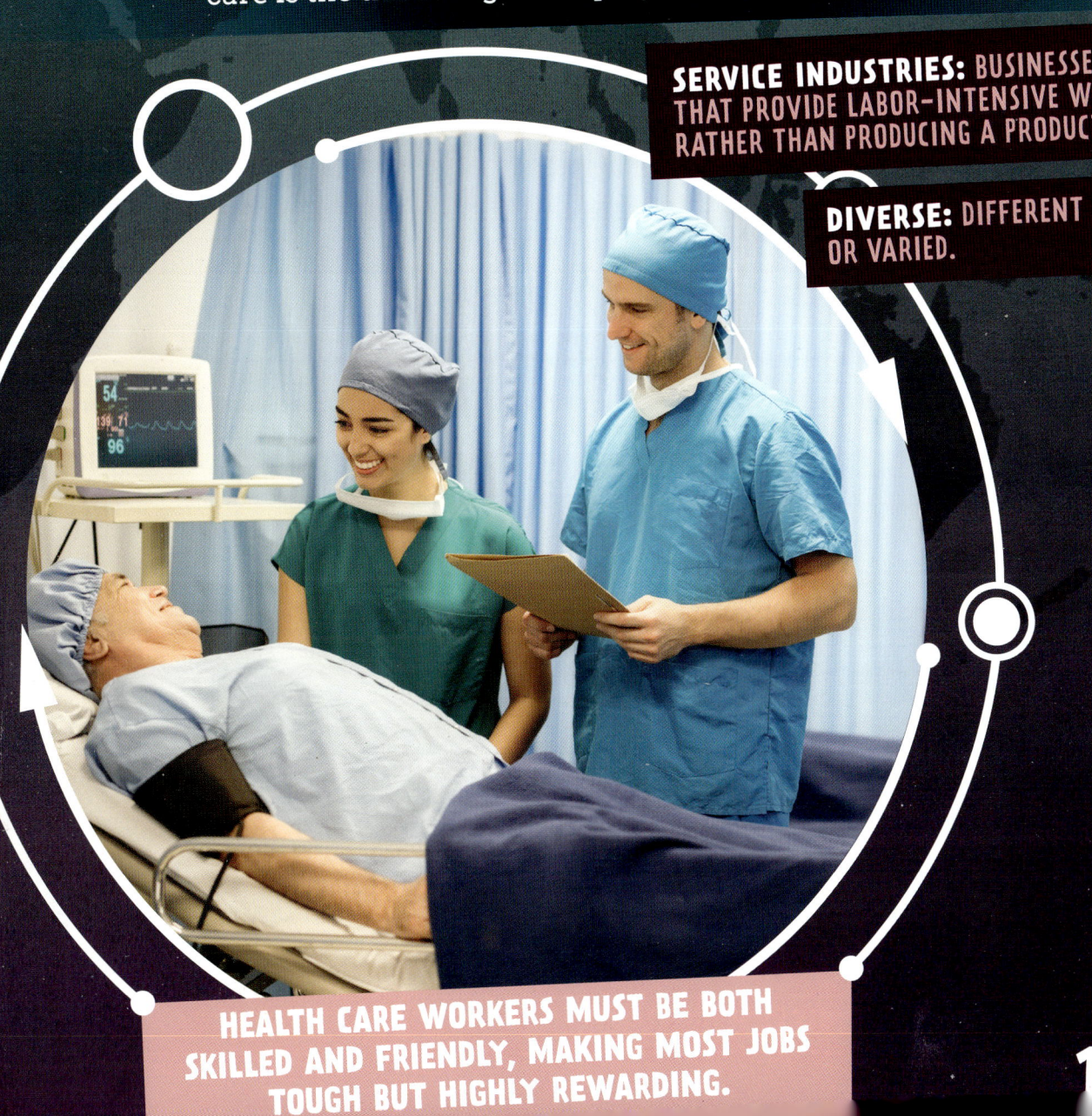

HEALTH CARE WORKERS MUST BE BOTH SKILLED AND FRIENDLY, MAKING MOST JOBS TOUGH BUT HIGHLY REWARDING.

A CHANGING RETAIL INDUSTRY

The growth of online shopping has significantly affected **retail industries** both within the United States and Canada and around the globe.

According to the U.S. Commerce Department, online retail—where customers shop at internet companies like Amazon—grew 300 percent between 2000 and 2018. Department store sales dropped almost 50 percent. A record number of retailers filed for bankruptcy, or ran out of money, in 2018, including stores like Toys "R" Us.

By 2020, internet retail is expected to reach $523 billion in the United States. The popularity of online shopping is expected to lead to the closure of many shopping malls throughout both countries. Websites allow U.S. and Canadian consumers to purchase directly from Chinese manufacturers, who often sell goods for cheaper prices, reducing the need for Canadian or American retailers.

FAST FACT

IN THE UNITED STATES, ALMOST 20 PERCENT OF ANNUAL RETAIL SALES TAKE PLACE BETWEEN BLACK FRIDAY—THE DAY AFTER THANKSGIVING—AND CHRISTMAS.

RETAIL INDUSTRIES: BUSINESSES THAT SELL DIRECTLY TO CONSUMERS.

RETAIL CHOICES

American and Canadian shoppers have a lot of choices in the retail industry, from cars to clothing to restaurants. The retail industry contains 4.8 million jobs in the United States and 2 million jobs in Canada. The largest retail category is in automobiles, followed by grocery stores, and then general merchandise. U.S. retail sales hit a record $6 trillion in 2018. Retailers get products directly from manufacturers in **wholesale industries**. In the United States, wholesaling is a $1.15 trillion industry.

STORES AND MALLS ARE SHUTTING DOWN ACROSS NORTH AMERICA AS RETAIL SALES MOVE TO THE INTERNET.

WHOLESALE INDUSTRIES: THE BUSINESS OF SELLING PRODUCTS TO RETAILERS.

THE IMPORTANCE OF MANUFACTURING

Factories may not be as important as they once were in the United States and Canada, but manufacturing still plays a vital role in both economies.

After China, the United States is the world's second-largest manufacturer. Manufacturing in the United States is a $2.2 trillion industry. Robots and increasing automation, or work done by machines, help make workers more productive.

Top manufactured products in the United States include plastics, automobiles, and petroleum products, such as gasoline. The United States leads the world in airplane manufacturing, with companies such as Boeing and Lockheed Martin producing a majority of the world's civilian aircraft.

Canada also has a large manufacturing field, mostly based in central Canada. Top manufactured products in Canada include lumber and paper, machinery, oil, steel, automobiles, and airplanes.

FAST FACT

SOME 12.75 MILLION AMERICANS WORK MANUFACTURING JOBS.

AMERICAN COMPANIES LIKE BOEING PRODUCE MOST OF THE WORLD'S CIVILIAN AIRCRAFT.

TECHNOLOGY AND CAPITAL GOODS

The United States's strength in technology helps it excel in creating **capital goods**. From the Wright Brothers' first successful airplane flight in 1903 to ongoing computer science research in Silicon Valley—an area of California—technological innovations gave America an advantage in capital goods. Today, the United States remains a leader in capital good creation, from airplanes to robots. Capital production declined after the 2008 recession because demand declined. Companies are not buying as much new equipment, and more are looking for opportunities overseas.

MOVING AWAY FROM AGRICULTURE

Agriculture in the United States and Canada is no longer as important as it used to be. Despite that, it remains a major industry in both countries, with a big impact on trade.

Only a small number of Americans and Canadians still work on farms. While 70 percent of American workers were once employed in agriculture in the 19th century, farmers and ranchers today make up only 2 percent of the American population.

However, the United States is still the world's largest agriculture exporter. It produces more food than the entire European Union. Canada, the fifth-largest exporter, exports $56 billion a year in agriculture and agri-food products. Corn is the biggest crop in the United States. In Canada, the largest crops are wheat and canola.

FAST FACT

THE MECHANICAL REAPER SPED UP THE PROCESS OF HARVESTING WHEAT.

THERE ARE 2.1 MILLION FARMS IN THE UNITED STATES. ABOUT 97 PERCENT OF THEM ARE FAMILY OWNED.

AGRICULTURE AND TECHNOLOGY

American and Canadian advancements in technology allow countries around the world to grow a large amount of food with fewer workers. This history of innovation stretches back to 1793, when Eli Whitney invented the cotton gin. The cotton gin sped up the process of removing seeds from cotton fiber, revolutionizing the production of cotton. In the 1830s, Cyrus McCormick's mechanical reaper sped up the process of harvesting wheat. Today, American and Canadian scientists are innovators in biotech crops and organic farming.

SCIENTIFIC DISCOVERIES

The United States has a long and successful history with scientific discovery, starting with Benjamin Franklin's experiments with electricity in 1752. Today, the United States is a global leader in scientific research. American scientists invented the steam engine, discovered DNA, performed the first human lung transplant, and proved that the universe is expanding.

Much of the United States's success in research comes from its support in funding. Much of that research funding—including biomedical research that leads to important developments in medicine and health care—comes from the private industry, including pharmaceutical, or drug, companies. The taxpayer-funded National Institutes of Health (NIH) also funds scientific research. Over the years, the NIH has supported 156 Nobel Prize winners.

FAST FACT

CANADA'S CONTRIBUTIONS TO SCIENTIFIC RESEARCH INCLUDE THE DISCOVERY OF INSULIN FOR THE TREATMENT OF DIABETES AND THE FIRST OPEN-HEART SURGERY.

ONE OF THE UNITED STATES'S BIGGEST—AND MOST CONTROVERSIAL—SCIENTIFIC DISCOVERIES WAS THE DEVELOPMENT OF THE ATOMIC BOMB.

POLITICS AND SCIENCE

Competition against other nations fueled some of the United States's biggest contributions in scientific discovery. During World War II, America led the successful effort to develop a functional atomic weapon, an undertaking known as the Manhattan Project. This atomic technology was an advantage in battle, allowing the United States to pull ahead in World War II. The U.S. conflict with the Soviet Union during the Cold War created the space race, leading to America's landing of astronauts on the moon in 1969.

TRADE AND COMMUNICATION

The United States is Canada's biggest trade partner. Every day, these North American neighbors exchange $1.9 billion in goods and services. In 2018, trade added up to $725 billion in goods and services between the two countries.

Canada is also the United States's largest supplier of energy. Three-quarters of Canadian exports go to the United States. This is partly because Canada shares a border with only the United States, making shipping goods to other countries more expensive.

Canada is one of the most trade-dependent countries in the world. In order to have enough goods and services, Canada needs to trade with other nations. Many Canadian goods come from the United States, including food, cars, electronics, books, and movies. Canada is the 12th-largest exporter in the world.

FAST FACT

THE UNITED STATES IS THE WORLD'S LARGEST IMPORTER, OR BUYER OF OTHER COUNTRIES' GOODS. IT'S THE WORLD'S SECOND-LARGEST TRADING NATION.

TECHNOLOGY AND COMMUNICATION

U.S. innovations in technology shaped how the world communicates. American inventors have been responsible for key developments in communication. In the 1830s, Samuel Morse's telegraph revolutionized long-distance communication by allowing people far away to communicate through Morse code. Other key communication technologies include Alexander Graham Bell's development of the phone and IBM's development of the personal computer. U.S. collaboration also led to the development of the Internet. Today, the United States is ranked as one of the countries most connected to the world.

THE INVENTION OF THE TELEGRAPH AND MORSE CODE REVOLUTIONIZED LONG-DISTANCE COMMUNICATION.

ETHICS AND THE ECONOMY

Ethics are an important part of keeping the free enterprise system functioning. When companies or individuals make unethical decisions, they can have harmful consequences.

That was the case in the United States in 2001 when a massive accounting fraud scheme collapsed the energy trading company Enron. The scheme, organized by the company's executives, caused an estimated $74 billion in losses. Thousands of Enron employees lost their pension funds.

Though businesses in the United States and Canada have sometimes hurt those countries' citizens, they are also the reason for their strong economies. The free enterprise–style systems in these nations allow entrepreneurs and scientists to follow their dreams, and make money doing so. Both countries hope to build on their shared history of scientific and economic strength well into the future.

FAST FACT

TO PREVENT ANOTHER ENRON SCANDAL, PUBLIC COMPANIES NOW HAVE TO FOLLOW NEW REGULATIONS AND LAWS FOR HOW THEY REPORT THEIR FINANCES.

THE FREE ENTERPRISE SYSTEM CAN'T WORK IF COMPANIES BEHAVE UNETHICALLY, AS ENRON DID IN THE EARLY 2000s.

PONZI SCHEMES COST BIG

Without ethics, scams and get-rich-quick schemes can negatively impact the American economy—and hurt individual people, as well. That includes Ponzi schemes: investment cons named after Charles Ponzi. These scams revolve around the process of paying old investors with money from new investors. American investment advisor and financier Bernie Madoff operated the longest-running and largest Ponzi scheme in history. Discovered in 2009, Madoff's scheme had thousands of victims. Madoff conned his clients for 20 years, causing losses of almost $65 billion.

GLOSSARY

capital goods: Products (such as factory equipment and tools) that are used to make other products.

communism: A way of organizing a society in which the government owns the things that are used to make and transport products (such as land, oil, factories, ships, etc.) and there is no privately owned property.

gross domestic product (GDP): The total value of the goods and services produced by the people of a nation during a year, not including the value of income earned in foreign countries.

immigrant: One who comes to a country to settle there.

inflation: A continual increase in the price of goods and services.

innovation: A new idea, device, or method.

profit: Money that is made in a business, through investing, etc., after all the costs and expenses are paid.

property: Something that is owned by a person or business.

recession: A period of time in which there is a decrease in economic activity and many people do not have jobs.

regulation: An official rule or law stating how something should be done.

socialism: A way of organizing a society in which major industries are owned and controlled by the government.

subsidize: To help someone or something pay for the costs of something.

venture capital: Money that is used to start a new business.

FOR MORE INFORMATION

BOOKS

DK Publishing. *The Economics Book: Big Ideas Simply Explained.* New York, NY: DK Publishing, 2018

Gigliotti, Jim. *Who Was Nikola Tesla?* New York, NY: Penguin Workshop, 2018.

Idzikowski, Lisa. *Globalization and Free Trade.* New York, NY: Greenhaven Publishing, 2018.

WEBSITES

BEA in the Classroom
www.bea.gov/resources/learning-center/bea-in-the-classroom
The U.S. Bureau of Economic Analysis's website offers handouts and interactive activities about the U.S. economy for teachers and students.

Bureau of Labor Statistics Student Page
www.bls.gov/k12
Student resources, quizzes, games, and a teacher's desk are available on the U.S. Bureau of Labor Statistics's site.

Money and Finance—Capitalism
www.ducksters.com/money/capitalism.php
Learn more about capitalism on this easy-to-follow webpage.

Publisher's note to educators and parents: Our editors have carefully reviewed these websites to ensure that they are suitable for students. Many websites change frequently, however, and we cannot guarantee that a site's future contents will continue to meet our high standards of quality and educational value. Be advised that students should be closely supervised whenever they access the internet.

INDEX

A
agriculture, 16, 22, 23

B
Boeing, 20, 21

C
coal, 10, 11

E
energy, 11, 26, 28
entrepreneur, 14, 15, 28

F
free enterprise, 6, 8, 9, 28, 29

G
Gross Domestic Product (GDP), 5, 16

H
health care, 16, 17, 24

I
inventions, 8, 13, 23, 24, 27
immigrants, 12, 13

J
Jobs, Steve, 15

L
labor, 8, 12, 16

M
manufacturing, 6, 16, 18, 19, 20

N
natural resources, 10, 11

O
online retail, 18

R
retail industry, 17, 18, 19

S
scientific innovations, 4, 12, 13, 23, 24, 25

T
trade, 9, 17, 22, 26

U
United States Federal Reserve, 9